Contents

Note about the story

Emily Brontë lived in the village of Haworth in Yorkshire, England, in the early 19th century. Her sisters were the writers Charlotte and Anne Brontë. *Wuthering Heights* was her only novel.

Class – what people did and how much money they had – was very important. Rich people were upper class. The men were "gentlemen", and their wives were "ladies". Teachers and doctors were middle class, and **servants*** and farm workers were lower class, or working class.

In the 19th century, women and men often married at a young age, and after they married the woman's money belonged to her husband.

Upper-class families usually lived in big houses. Often, the servants who lived and worked in the house had their own kitchen and rooms. The house had a **housekeeper** – a woman who looked after the house and the family who lived in it. It often had several very large gardens around it and farmland that men and boys came each day to work on.

Sometimes, a rich man owned more than one house. A **tenant** could pay money, or "rent", to a **landlord** to live in his second house for a number of months or years. This was called a **tenancy**.

English weather can change very quickly – in spring, it can be sunny one day, and snowy the next. This happens often in wild places like the Yorkshire **moors**.

*Definitions of words in **bold** can be found in the glossary on pages 92–95.

Before-reading questions

1 What do you know about Yorkshire in England? Write your answer in your notebook.

2 One of the people in the story is called a "cuckoo". Find information about this bird.

3 Read the "Note about the story" on page 4. In the 19th century in England, women gave their money to their husbands after they married. Did women do this in your country, too? Do they do this now?

4 Do you have class in your country? If the answer is yes, how do upper-class people in your country live? How do middle-class and working-class people live?

5 Read the back cover of the book. Are these sentences *true* or *false*?
   a The family in the story live in a city.
   b It is summer in Yorkshire, England.
   c Catherine lived in the house years before.

CHAPTER ONE
A new tenant

1801 – Two days ago, I visited my new **landlord**, Mr Heathcliff, at Wuthering Heights. I rode across the **moor** in a cold November wind that carried bits of snow. I was feeling excited about meeting the other man who lived in this wild place. I hoped we would find a lot to talk about.

He was standing at the front of the house when I arrived. As I walked up the path, he put his hands in his pockets and stared at me with angry, black eyes. He was tall, with black hair and dark skin, and his clothes were expensive. They were the clothes of a gentleman.

"Mr Heathcliff?" I said.

He nodded his head but did not smile.

"I am Mr Lockwood, your new **tenant**, **sir**. I have just moved into Thrushcross Grange. I want to introduce myself."

"Come in!" said Mr Heathcliff, but he said it quickly, and he did not seem happy to see me. Then he shouted, "Joseph, take Mr Lockwood's horse and get a **jug** of **wine**."

A **servant** appeared from a door. He was a very old man, with thin arms and legs. I reached out my hand to him, but he did not shake it. He had an angry look in his eyes.

As I followed my landlord into the large house with its thick stone walls and thin windows, I noticed the date 1500 and the name "Hareton Earnshaw" above the door. I knew that "wuthering" was a **Yorkshire** word meaning "the **blowing** of the wind on the moor". Because I have now seen how high the house stands on the moor, I understand its strange name. I wanted to ask Mr Heathcliff more about Wuthering Heights, but his unfriendly look made me stay quiet. I followed him into a huge, **bare** kitchen with a **dresser** at one end that had lots of plates on it.

A long wooden table stood in the middle of the kitchen with three tall chairs around it. A fire burned at one end. It had a row of old guns above it. The floor was made of bare white stone, and in the corner lay a dog. She **growled** at me if I came near.

A young woman sat in a wooden chair at one side of the fire, and a young man sat opposite her. The woman was **slim**, with a beautiful face and blonde hair. When she saw me, she did not smile but got tiredly to her feet.

"Get some tea," said Mr Heathcliff.

"Is he having some?" she asked, pointing at me.

"Just get it!" he said, quickly.

She put some tea and bread in front of us. At that moment, the young man also stood up and came to join us at the table. He looked like a servant in his old clothes, and his hands were brown and **rough**, like a farm worker's.

"Who are these people?" I thought to myself as we ate. "Is this beautiful woman the wife of Mr Heathcliff? Or is she married to this younger man?"

"It has started snowing outside," said Mr Heathcliff, suddenly. "Why did you come to visit in weather like this, Mr Lockwood?"

I got up from the table and walked to the window. Outside, the sky was now black, and the air was thick with snow. It fell on to the garden and low stone walls. Around the house, the moor was slowly turning white.

"I will need someone to help me find my way home," I said, "or I will get **lost**."

"Take the road that brought you here," replied the woman. "That is the best advice that I can give you."

I turned to Mr Heathcliff. "Could your son–"

"He is not my son," said Mr Heathcliff, quickly, and

laughed. "Hareton, go with Joseph and put those sheep in the barn before the snow covers them."

"But how will I get home?" I asked the woman again as Hareton and Joseph left.

"Who do you want to take you home?" she replied. "I can't go. They will not let me. There is Mr Heathcliff, Earnshaw, Zillah the **housekeeper** and Joseph. But none of them will take you."

"Are there any boys who work on the farm? Could one of them take me home?"

"No," she replied.

"Then I must stay here," I said. "I can't ride alone on the moor in this snow."

"Then learn it as a lesson!" shouted Mr Heathcliff. "You have to plan journeys on this moor in winter. I don't have rooms for guests. If you want to stay, you must share a bed with Hareton or Joseph."

When I heard this, I felt very angry with Mr Heathcliff, and I wanted to leave Wuthering Heights immediately. I got up and pushed past him. Throwing open the kitchen door, I walked into the garden to find Joseph holding a **lantern**. I immediately pulled it from his hand. "I'll bring it back tomorrow!" I said.

"Mr Heathcliff! Mr Heathcliff! He's stealing the lantern!" shouted Joseph. "Get him, Gnasher! Get him, Wolf!" The next moment, I heard growling, and then I felt some dogs on me, pulling me down. I could not move until Mr Heathcliff pulled them off me. Then I jumped up quickly, feeling angry and frightened. Suddenly, my nose began to **bleed**. I heard Mr Heathcliff laugh, and then a woman's voice said, "What is going to happen next, Mr Heathcliff? Are we murdering people in our own garden now? Look at this **poor** man. Come inside now, and I'll stop that bleeding."

I guessed that this large lady with the kind voice was the housekeeper, Zillah. She immediately pulled me back into the kitchen and sat me down in a chair. Then, she held my nose hard. I felt sick and **confused**, and I knew I would have to stay at Wuthering Heights. I could not ride home on the moor feeling like this. Mr Heathcliff ordered Zillah to get me a glass of wine, and then he went into another room. I sat down until I felt a bit better, and then Zillah took me upstairs.

CHAPTER TWO
A ghost in the night

As she led me, Zillah told me to cover the lantern and stay quiet. "He has strange ideas about this room," she said, opening a door. "He doesn't let people sleep there, but I don't know why. I've only lived here for a couple of years. A lot of strange things happen in this house."

I was too tired and shocked to be interested at that moment. She showed me a small, bare room that had a chair and a small bed next to the only window. Then, she closed the door and left me.

I immediately got into bed and put my lantern on the window **ledge**. The ledge had a few old books at one end, and someone had **scratched** some words in its paint: *Catherine Earnshaw, Catherine Heathcliff, Catherine Linton.*

I quickly fell asleep and had many strange dreams before I was slowly woken by the sound of a branch knocking on the glass of the window. I sat up and tried to open it, but the window would not move. Feeling tired and angry, I pushed harder, and suddenly my hand went through the glass. But instead of a branch, a small, cold hand closed around mine. Then a girl's voice cried, "Let me in! Let me in!"

I suddenly felt very frightened. "Who are you?" I asked and tried to pull my hand free, but those cold fingers held it hard. "Catherine Linton," the voice replied. "I've been lost on the moor, but I'm home now!"

"Let me go, and I will let you in," I said, and the fingers relaxed. I pulled back my hand quickly and pushed the pile of books across the ledge in front of the broken window. "I'll never let you in!" I shouted. "Not in twenty years."

"It's been twenty years," cried the voice. "I've been lost on the moor for twenty years!" These words were followed by a scratching sound, and then the books began to move forward on the window ledge.

I jumped out of bed and screamed. The next moment, there was the sound of a man's feet coming quickly towards my bedroom door, before it was pushed open. Then, Mr Heathcliff came into the room with a lantern and said quietly, "Is anyone here?"

I stood up. "It is only your guest, sir," I said. "I had a bad dream, and it made me scream. I'm sorry if I woke you, but this room is full of ghosts. I understand now why you keep it locked. That crazy woman – what is she called? Catherine Linton, or Earnshaw? She said she'd been on the moor for twenty years!"

When he heard this, he closed his eyes and **groaned**. Then, a tear ran slowly down his face, and I immediately felt very angry with myself because of course he knew the woman. I remembered the other name I had seen scratched in the paint: "*Catherine Heathcliff*".

Mr Heathcliff opened his eyes. "Mr Lockwood, you can sleep in my room. I will not sleep now."

I took the lantern and left the room, and then I heard something that made me stop. I turned to see Mr Heathcliff getting on to the bed and pushing open the window. Then, he cried out into the night, "Catherine, do come. Oh, do come once more!" But there was nothing outside but the snow and blowing wind.

I went downstairs quickly and found a chair near the fire in the kitchen. I sat down on it and finally went back to sleep. When I woke it was morning, and there were voices. Zillah was making a new fire, while the younger woman sat next to her in a chair next to the dresser and read a book. Mr Heathcliff was standing with his back towards me, and he was shouting at Zillah. Then, he turned to the young woman and said, "And there you are, doing nothing again. Everyone in this house works for their food and bed!"

"You can shout, but I will do nothing," the woman replied, tiredly. She put down her book and stood up. The next moment, Mr Heathcliff lifted a hand, but she jumped away from him to a safe corner. I moved forward quickly, and Mr Heathcliff put his hands in his pockets. He knew that he could not hit a woman in front of a guest.

I did not wait to have breakfast with them, but quickly rode my horse home through the snow. Mr Heathcliff led me most of the way without speaking. When we got to Thrushcross Grange, he left me and turned back to Wuthering Heights. The worried servants were waiting for me, but I did not speak to them. Instead, I went straight to bed feeling **weak** and sick.

CHAPTER THREE
At Thrushcross Grange

This morning, I stayed in my bedroom and saw no one. But when evening came I began to feel better, so I came downstairs. I called for Nelly Dean, my housekeeper, and asked her to make a fire and bring me dinner.

"You have lived here a long time, haven't you?" I asked, after she had put a bowl of soup in front of me. I knew that she liked to talk, and I wanted to know about the people at Wuthering Heights.

"Yes, sir," she replied. "I've lived here for eighteen years. I came when Miss Catherine was married. Her husband employed me as his housekeeper after she died."

"You've seen many changes," I said.

"I have," she replied. "And a lot of trouble, too."

I was quiet for a moment, thinking about the beautiful young woman I had met at Wuthering Heights. "Tell me," I said. "Why does Mr Heathcliff prefer to live at Wuthering Heights when Thrushcross Grange is a much better house? Does he need the money?"

"Need the money?" she replied. "No, Mr Heathcliff is very rich, and he becomes richer every year. But if he can make more money from having a tenant at Thrushcross Grange, then he will."

"Has he got children?" I asked.

"He had a son, but he is dead now."

"And the young woman. Who is she?"

"She is Cathy – the daughter of Miss Catherine Earnshaw. Miss Catherine married Mr Edgar Linton, who used to own Thrushcross Grange. I looked after Cathy, the poor little thing!" she replied.

"And the boy, Hareton?"

"He is Cathy's cousin," she said, "the son of Miss Catherine's brother, Hindley."

"They're a big family, aren't they? I'm a bit confused."

"Yes, sir."

"I saw that Wuthering Heights has 'Hareton Earnshaw' and the date 1500 written above the door. Are they an old family?"

"Yes, sir, they are a very old family," she said. "And Hareton is the last of them. Wuthering Heights should be his, not Mr Heathcliff's. That poor boy has been **tricked**, but he doesn't know it." She stopped speaking for a moment, then said, "Mr Heathcliff is a difficult man, isn't he?"

I smiled at her. "Yes, he's a rough and angry man, with a bad **temper**."

"A *very* bad temper," she replied.

"What terrible thing has happened in his life to make him like that?" I asked.

"It's a sad story, sir. Mr Heathcliff is the **cuckoo** who pushed the others out of their **nest**. I will tell you about it."

And then she sat down in front of the fire she had just made and began to tell me her story.

———

It started many years ago, when I was a small child. Before I came to live here, I lived at Wuthering Heights. My mother looked after Hindley Earnshaw, and I used to play with him and his sister, Catherine. One summer afternoon, Hindley's father left for Liverpool. He was gone for three days, and the children missed him a lot. On the third night, they did not go to bed. They waited in the sitting room for him to return.

At 11 p.m., the door opened, and Mr Earnshaw came in and fell back into a chair. Then, he opened his big coat and cried, "Look at this, wife. I've never carried anything so heavy in my life, but we must see it as a gift from **God**."

Catherine and Hindley moved forward, and above Catherine's head I saw a dirty, black-haired child. He was big enough to walk, and his face looked the same age as Catherine's. But when he spoke, it was in a language that no one could understand.

At first, Mrs Earnshaw was very angry. "How will we feed him when we have our own children to look after?" she shouted at her husband. But Mr Earnshaw was a very kind man. He said that the boy had been hungry and alone, and no one knew whose child he was. He could not leave the boy like that, he said, and he wanted him to become part of the family. Then, he asked me to wash the boy and let him sleep with Hindley and Catherine.

The Earnshaws called him "Heathcliff" – it was the name of a son who had died. It has always been both his first and last name.

Heathcliff was a quiet, **moody** child, but Mr Earnshaw loved him, and he became Mr Earnshaw's favourite. Heathcliff and Catherine quickly became close, and they played together all the time. But Hindley hated Heathcliff, and he used to **tease** him and hit him. Heathcliff's face was often **bruised**. When Mrs Earnshaw became ill and died two years after Heathcliff arrived, Hindley teased and hit the boy even more.

Then, when Catherine and Heathcliff were around thirteen years old, Mr Earnshaw also became ill. He slowly became very thin and weak, and he changed. He wasn't gentle and kind now – he was silent and moody, and sometimes he had a terrible temper. He thought that everyone hated him for bringing Heathcliff to the house, and he did not want to hear bad things said about the boy. Of course, his father's love for Heathcliff made Hindley hate Heathcliff even more. Finally, Mr Earnshaw became tired of Hindley's bad temper and Heathcliff's bruised face. He decided to send Hindley to college.

I hoped that life would be quieter after that, but I was wrong. The problem was Catherine. She was a very naughty, wild child, but she also had very beautiful dark eyes and a sweet smile. She loved Heathcliff too much and spent all her time with him. She liked to tease her father that she had more **power** over Heathcliff than he did. As her father grew weaker, she became even naughtier, until one night Mr Earnshaw lost his temper and said, "I cannot love you, Catherine. You are worse than your brother!" This made her cry at first, but, when I told her to say sorry to her father, she laughed.

A few weeks after he had lost his temper with Catherine, Mr Earnshaw was sitting by the fire in the evening. As the wind blew around the house, Catherine sat against her father's knees, and Heathcliff lay on the floor with his head on her legs. "I will sing you to sleep, Daddy," Catherine said. Then, she began to sing softly, and Mr Earnshaw's head slowly dropped on to his chest.

A few minutes later, Catherine touched him on the shoulder, but he did not move. Then, she stood up and, putting her arms around his neck, immediately screamed,

"Oh, he's dead, Heathcliff! He's dead!" The two children began to cry, and I began to cry with them. Then, Joseph told me to go and get the doctor from Gimmerton. I ran over the moor through the blowing wind and rain, and I brought the doctor back with me. When I went upstairs, Catherine and Heathcliff were in their room, but they were not in their beds. They were sitting close together on the floor, speaking beautifully about God and **heaven**. They did not need me, because they had each other.

CHAPTER FOUR
Hindley returns from college

Mr Hindley came home for his father's **funeral** and surprised us by bringing a young wife with him. He never told us where Frances was from, probably because she had no money. I'm sure that this was why Mr Earnshaw never knew about her. He was a gentleman and had not wanted his son to marry a poor woman.

Mr Hindley had changed a lot. He spoke and dressed differently, and, as soon as he returned, he told me and Joseph that we must stay in the servants' kitchen and rooms. He and his wife would live in the other part of the house.

His wife was happy to find a sister in the house, and she quickly became friends with Catherine. At first, she ran around with her and gave her presents. But she did not like Catherine's love for Heathcliff, and soon she spoke about it to Mr Hindley. Mr Hindley became angry, and he told Heathcliff to live with the servants. He said that Heathcliff would not get any more lessons and would have to work out on the fields with the farm boys instead.

At first, Heathcliff was still happy, because Catherine taught him what she learned and still played with him all the time. The two of them were always running around the moor, but Mr Hindley was only interested in his wife. He never saw Heathcliff and Catherine together and did not realize how rough and wild they were becoming.

Late one evening, about five weeks before Christmas, Heathcliff came home alone. I was waiting worriedly in the kitchen and ran to meet him at the door. "Where is Miss Catherine?" I cried. "Has she had an accident?"

"She's at Thrushcross Grange," he replied. "And I wanted to be there, too, but they did not want me to stay."

"Why were you at Thrushcross Grange?" I asked, leading him into the kitchen.

"Catherine and I were walking on the moor," he replied, "and we saw the lights of Thrushcross Grange. So, we climbed into the gardens and looked through the sitting-room window. Oh, but it's a beautiful place, Nelly – the gardens are huge, and you should see the paintings and furniture! Mr and Mrs Linton weren't in the room. There were two children there – Edgar Linton and his sister, Isabella. They were alone, and they were fighting over a little dog! We laughed at them. When do Catherine and I ever fight over things? But we were laughing, and I think Mr and Mrs Linton heard us. They came and opened the door, so we ran away. But then we heard a loud growl – they had sent a huge dog after us – and it brought Catherine down by the ankle. Then a servant called the dog off her.

"Mrs Linton came forward with Edgar and stared at Catherine. 'That's Miss Earnshaw,' Edgar said to his mother. 'But look at the blood on her ankle.'

"'Miss Earnshaw?' said Mrs Linton. 'On the moor at this time of night? Does her brother know about this? And who is this boy – is he the one from Liverpool?'

"I started shouting at all of them," Heathcliff told me, "but the servants pulled me away while the Lintons carried Catherine into the house and shut the door. I watched through the window as they put her on the sofa and took her coat off. Then they gave her food and brushed her beautiful hair."

"Mr Hindley will not be happy about this, Heathcliff," I said.

Those words were truer than I thought. The next day, Mr Linton came to the house and spoke to Mr Hindley about how badly he was looking after his family. It made Hindley feel stupid. He did not hit Heathcliff, but he told him not to speak to Miss Catherine again. If he did, then he must leave Wuthering Heights.

Miss Catherine stayed at Thrushcross Grange for five weeks. By Christmas, her ankle was better, so she rode home with Mr Linton. She had changed a lot, and she dressed and acted very differently. Hindley helped her down from her horse and brought her inside. "Catherine, you are a lady now, and you are beautiful," he said. "She is much more beautiful than Isabella Linton, isn't she, Frances?"

"Yes, she is," agreed Frances. "But she must not become wild again."

I took off her coat and saw her beautiful dress and new shoes. When the dogs ran up to her, she did not touch them. She was worried that they would make her clothes dirty.

"Where is Heathcliff?" she asked, immediately.

No one had tried to look after Heathcliff much before

Catherine went to Thrushcross Grange, but no one had tried at all while she was there. Now, his clothes were covered in dirt, and his hair had not been brushed for weeks.

He slowly came forward, and she put her arms around him and kissed him. Then, she moved away from him and laughed. "Why are you so angry?" she asked.

"Shake hands with Catherine," said Hindley.

"I won't!" said the boy. "I won't be laughed at!"

"I'm sorry!" said Catherine. "I didn't mean to laugh at you, but you look strange. Maybe it's because I'm used to Edgar and Isabella Linton. If you wash your face and brush your hair, then you will look fine, but you are so dirty!"

"You don't have to touch me," replied Heathcliff. "If I want to be dirty, then I will be!" And he ran out of the room.

CHAPTER FIVE
Catherine has to choose

In June the next year, Hindley and Frances had a son, Hareton. But, sadly, Frances became ill and died shortly after having the baby. I had to look after the new baby, because Hindley was going mad with **grief** over his wife's death. He did not cry, but his temper became terrible, and he began to drink a lot of wine. He shouted at everything and everyone, and most of the servants and farm boys left. Only Joseph and I stayed. He lost his temper most with Heathcliff, but the young man seemed to enjoy watching Hindley's pain, and he often teased him. This made Hindley even more angry.

Catherine was fifteen now. She was slim and beautiful, but she was also a proud and **spoiled** girl. I did not like her much, but she continued to like me. Heathcliff still loved her, and, although Edgar Linton was wealthy and handsome, he found it hard to make Catherine love him as much as she loved Heathcliff.

———

Nelly pointed to the wall. "That is Edgar Linton's picture on the wall," she said. "His wife's picture used to be next to it, but Mr Heathcliff took it."

Nelly lifted the lantern. I saw a man's soft, worried face. It looked a lot like the face of the young woman who I had met at Wuthering Heights.

"He's handsome," I said.

"He looked better when he was happy," she replied. Then Nelly returned to the story.

———

After Miss Catherine came back to Wuthering Heights, she continued to see the Lintons. When Edgar and Isabella came to visit her, she was a lady – polite and quiet – but with her family she was a different person. She was still proud and wild.

Edgar and Heathcliff hated each other, of course, and Catherine could not decide who she liked the most. One afternoon, when Hindley was away and I was in the kitchen with Hareton, she asked me for advice. "Oh, Nelly," she said, "I'm so unhappy!"

"Why," I asked, "when you have everything you want and so many friends?"

"Please, can you keep a secret for me?" she asked.

"If it's important, I can," I replied.

"It is, Nelly; I don't know what to do! Edgar Linton has asked me to marry him, and I have said yes – but was I right?" she cried, and she put her hands together.

"Well, there are many things to think about," I said. "First of all, do you love Edgar Linton?"

"Of course I do," she replied.

"Why do you love him?"

She looked surprised. "I just . . . do. He is handsome and rich, and nice to be with."

"That's not good enough!" I said.

"And he will be very rich, and I will be the richest woman in the area. I love the ground under his feet and the air over his head. I love everything that he touches and every word that he says."

"You love him because he is handsome and rich. So, what are you unhappy about?"

She was quiet for a moment, and then she said, "Nelly, sometimes I have a dream. I dream that I am dead and in heaven, and I am crying because I want to come back to earth. Suddenly, I am thrown back on the moor, and I wake up feeling so happy because I am back at Wuthering Heights. That is my secret. I should not marry Edgar, and if my brother was kinder to Heathcliff, I would marry Heathcliff instead. But I cannot marry him, Nelly, because he is not rich or a gentleman. Heathcliff will never know how much I love him. I am Heathcliff. He is more myself than I am. Our **souls** are made from the same thing, while Linton is as different from me as water from fire."

As she was speaking, I turned my head and saw Heathcliff quietly leaving the kitchen. He had only stayed long enough to hear Catherine say that she could not marry him because he was below her. But Catherine had not seen him.

"What is it?" said Catherine, nervously, seeing me look towards the door.

"I think Heathcliff was listening to us from behind the door," I said. "I didn't know he was here."

"Oh no, did he hear me?" she cried. "He didn't, did he? He doesn't know what being in love is."

"Why shouldn't he know?" I replied. "When you become Edgar Linton's wife, he will lose his friend, his love and everything that is important to him. Do you know how you will feel when you are not together?"

"But we will always be together," she cried. "If anyone tries to **part** us, I will be very angry!"

"I do not think your husband will feel that way," I said. "And I think that you are being very stupid. Please don't tell me any more of your secrets, because I won't keep them."

At that moment, Joseph entered the kitchen. Catherine picked up Hareton and took him to a corner.

"Where's Heathcliff?" Joseph asked. "He should be back from the fields now."

"I'll look for him," I said. I went out and called, but there was no answer. As the hours passed, Catherine grew more and more worried. "Where is he, Nelly?" she kept asking.

"Did he hear what I said? Why doesn't he come home?" Then, she went out on to the moor to look for him.

At midnight, a storm came. Finally, I took Hareton upstairs and slept. When I came down in the morning, Catherine was sitting alone in the kitchen, and she was crying. Her clothes and hair were very wet, and her whole body was shaking.

Hindley came down the stairs behind me and immediately went to her. "She's ill," said her brother, taking her hand. "Why did you go out into the storm, Catherine?"

"Heathcliff has gone," cried Catherine. "You wanted him to go. But now you don't have to make him go, because he's already gone, he's gone!"

I was too busy looking after Hareton to nurse Catherine, so, when she was a bit better, Mrs Linton took her to Thrushcross Grange. Sadly, Mr and Mrs Linton then caught Catherine's illness, and they both died while she was staying with them.

Catherine finally came back to Wuthering Heights, and she seemed well again, although she said it was because of me that Heathcliff had gone. She stopped speaking to me and stayed away from her brother. The doctor said we must let her do what she wanted or she would lose her temper, and that would be bad for her **health**.

On a sunny day in March, about three years after Heathcliff left Wuthering Heights, Edgar Linton married Catherine at Gimmerton Church. He was the happiest man alive, and she seemed happy, too. He then asked me to come to work for him at Thrushcross Grange and said that he would pay me a lot of money. Hareton was now five years old. I loved him, but I had to leave him with his father, Hindley, and without a woman in the house to help him. I was not happy about this, because Hindley was still drinking every day, and Wuthering Heights was a sad and rough place for a small child to live in. I'm sure Hareton has now forgotten everything about Nelly Dean who loved him so much.

———————

At this moment, the housekeeper looked towards the clock and was surprised to see it was 1.30 a.m. She got up quickly to go to bed, and, as I was tired too, I did not try to stop her. I could wait to hear the next part of her story.

CHAPTER SIX
Heathcliff becomes a gentleman

Now, I am ill. Oh, this terrible winter! I am tired of these dark skies and great snowy moor! The doctor told me it might be spring before I can go outside again. But I am happy that I have Nelly Dean to listen to. She brings my **medicine** to me daily, and each time she tells me a little more of her story.

––––––––––

At first, Catherine seemed to love Mr Linton a lot. Sometimes, she was quiet and a bit sad. But she was mostly happy, and because of this so was he. I thought they were going to be really happy, but then it ended.

One warm evening in September, six months after Catherine and Edgar were married, I was coming from the garden with some apples when I heard a voice say, "Nelly, is that you?"

I turned to see a tall man in dark, expensive clothes, with a dark face and hair. He looked very different – like a gentleman – but his eyes were the same.

"What?" I said. "Is it really *you*?"

I went to the sitting room and told Mr and Mrs Linton that an old friend had come to visit. Catherine quickly went out to the hall, then came back a few minutes later and took her husband's hands in hers.

"Oh, Edgar, Edgar!" she cried, excitedly. "Heathcliff is back!"

A few minutes later, Heathcliff entered the room. He sat down opposite Catherine, and they looked at each other with bright, excited eyes, while Mr Linton's face was worried. "Oh, Heathcliff, this is like a dream!" cried Catherine. Suddenly, she jumped forward and took his hands in hers. "You have been gone for three years, and you never thought of me once!"

"No more than you thought of me!" replied Heathcliff, roughly.

"Catherine, please come to the table," said her husband, and I could see he was very unhappy. "Nelly, please make us some tea. Mr Heathcliff will have a long walk home tonight, and I am thirsty."

"Are you staying at Gimmerton?" I asked Mr Heathcliff when he was leaving later that evening.

"No," he replied, surprising me. "Hindley has invited me to stay at Wuthering Heights because we played **cards** this morning, and I won. Now he knows that I have money, he's happy for me to come again."

During the next five months, Heathcliff – or Mr Heathcliff, I should say now – started visiting Catherine at Thrushcross Grange. At first, it was not very often, and they were quieter and both more careful about showing their feelings now. This made Mr Linton relax for a while, but then something happened that made him worry even more.

Isabella Linton seemed to like Mr Heathcliff. She was

eighteen years old, slim and pretty. Her brother loved her a lot, and he did not trust Mr Heathcliff. Yes, Heathcliff had money now, and expensive clothes, but Mr Linton knew that he was not a gentleman. He had not changed inside.

One cold evening in January, Catherine was in the garden when she found Mr Heathcliff and Isabella under the trees, kissing. Then Isabella turned and quickly walked away.

"What are you doing, Heathcliff?" cried Catherine. "If Mr Linton hears about this, he will stop you coming here!"

"Let him try!" replied Mr Heathcliff, angrily. "Every day I hate him more."

"Stop it!" cried Catherine. "Why did you kiss her? Or did she come and kiss you first?"

"Why do you care?" Mr Heathcliff shouted. "I can kiss her if she wants to kiss me. I am not your husband, so you can't stop me! You have **betrayed** me, Catherine, and if you think that I don't know it, then you are stupid. You can't trick me with sweet words. I will get my **revenge** on you."

"You have changed so much!" cried Catherine. "How have I betrayed you? But if you want to get revenge on me, then yes, kiss my husband's sister and fight with him about it. That will work."

When Mr Linton heard about Mr Heathcliff and his sister, he was very angry, and he told Isabella that Mr Heathcliff could not come again.

After this, Isabella was very unhappy. Catherine was also very angry, because she could not see Heathcliff. She stayed in her room and would not speak to her husband. Then, she stopped eating, and I could see that she was becoming ill. One stormy night in early February, when the wind was blowing hard over the moor, she asked me to throw open the windows so that she could see Wuthering Heights. I was so worried that I called the doctor.

"She can get better," he said, "but she needs peace."

But, the following morning, a terrible thing happened. One of the servant girls had gone to Gimmerton, and when she returned home she came into the sitting room crying, "Miss Isabella's gone! She's gone! Mr Heathcliff has run away with her."

"That cannot be true!" said Mr Linton, standing up. "It cannot. What has given you that strange idea? Nelly, please go to look for her."

"It is, it is," replied the girl. "I met a boy on the road – he brings the milk here. He said that last night he was on the road not long after midnight, and he saw Mr Heathcliff and Miss Isabella in a **carriage** two miles away from Gimmerton. The woman had a big coat and a hat on, but he knew it was Miss Linton. Then the carriage drove away quickly. Everyone's talking about it in Gimmerton."

I ran straight into Isabella's room, but she wasn't there. I found Mr Linton sitting by Catherine's bed, while his wife slept. When he looked up and saw my face, he knew he did not have to ask where his sister was.

"Shall we try to follow her and bring her back?" I asked. But Mr Linton shook his head.

"No," he said. "She chose to go. We will not talk about her again."

CHAPTER SEVEN
Catherine's last goodbye

It was a dark winter's night, and we were both sitting in front of the fire at Thrushcross Grange. I was feeling a little better, but I was still weak. Nelly continued to tell me her story.

———

Mr Heathcliff and Miss Linton stayed away for six weeks. During that time, Catherine became very ill. But Mr Linton stayed with her and nursed her day and night, and by March she had slowly started to get better. Finally, she was able to leave her bedroom and come downstairs. I lit a fire for her, and she sat in a chair by the window staring out at the moor.

Four weeks after they had left, Isabella wrote a short note to her brother. It told him that she and Heathcliff were married. Edgar did not reply. Then, two weeks after that, I got a longer letter from her.

Dear Nelly,

Five days ago I came to Wuthering Heights and heard that Catherine is ill. I hope that she is getting better.

Nelly, I miss Edgar and want to see his face again more than anything. As soon as I left Thrushcross

Grange, I wanted to come back. Nelly, how did you live at Wuthering Heights? And who is Heathcliff? Is he a man?

It was evening when Heathcliff and I arrived at Wuthering Heights. Joseph came out. What a rude man! The first thing he did was lift a lantern up to my face, and then he gave me an angry look and turned away. He took our horses, and Heathcliff stayed to talk to him while I entered the house – what a bare and dirty place!

On my first night here, Heathcliff left me at the house and went out. Joseph and Hareton would not show me to our bedroom, because Mr Heathcliff had the key. I had to sleep in a chair in the kitchen until Heathcliff woke me in the morning. He had learned that Catherine was ill. He said she was ill because of my brother. He hates Edgar because Edgar married Catherine, and he wants to make me unhappy and hurt me so that he hurts Edgar.

I am now living here. I have met Hindley Earnshaw, who drinks too much and seems unhappy and crazy. He hates Heathcliff and says it is because Heathcliff has taken his money from him. His son, Hareton, is rough and wild.

Nelly, I hate Heathcliff! I have been stupid, and I am so unhappy. Please do not tell anyone at Thrushcross Grange what has happened.

Yours,
ISABELLA

As soon as I got this letter, I went to see Mr Linton and told him that his sister was at Wuthering Heights. "She wants you to forgive her," I said.

"Forgive her!" shouted Mr Linton. "I cannot forgive her, Nelly, and I do not want to see her."

"Can't you just write her a little note, sir?" I asked.

"No," he answered. "I do not want to talk to anyone in Heathcliff's family."

On the Sunday that followed Isabella and Heathcliff's return, all the family and servants, except Catherine, went to church. Although it was early spring, the weather was warm, so I left the doors open. Catherine sat next to the window in her bedroom in a long white dress, with her thick hair over her shoulders. Being ill had made her different. She was calm, and her eyes were dreamy and sad.

Suddenly, there was the sound of feet entering the hall below. Catherine quickly turned and looked towards the door with excited eyes. He did not find the room immediately, but walked up and down until she asked me to let him in. The next second, he was by her side and holding her in his arms.

"Oh Catherine, oh, you are my life!" he cried.

"What will happen now, Heathcliff?" she replied. "You and Edgar have broken my heart. I am not sorry for you! You have killed me, and you are happy because of it. You are so well and strong. How many years will you live after I have gone?"

Heathcliff held her closer. Then, he tried to rise, but she caught his hair in her hand and pulled him down. "I wish that I could hold you until we were both dead!" she cried. "I don't care about your pain. Will you forget me? Will you be happy when I am under the ground? Will you love another woman and have many children, and in twenty years will you come to my **grave** and say, 'There lies Catherine Earnshaw. I loved her once and was sorry to lose her, but she has gone now.' Will you say this, Heathcliff?"

"You will make me as mad as you!" he shouted, pulling his head away. "How can you talk like that? Don't you realize that I will always remember these words? I have not killed you. *You* have killed yourself. Oh, Catherine, why did you betray your own heart?" And suddenly her arm was around his neck, and her face was against his, and they were both crying.

"Why did you marry Linton, Catherine?" he went on. "Yes, you can kiss me and make me kiss you and cry. You *loved* me, so why did you leave me for him and your weak love? No one could part us – but *you* did. I have not broken your heart. *You* have broken it, and now mine is broken, too. What kind of life will I have without you in it?"

"Let me go, let me go!" cried Catherine. "If I have done something wrong, then I am dying for it now. You left me, too, but I am not angry with you. Forgive me!"

"It is hard to forgive and look into these eyes and feel these thin hands," he answered. "Kiss me again and don't let me see your eyes. I forgive you for what you have done to me." They were quiet then, their faces together and wet from crying.

I watched them worriedly. It was late afternoon now. "Mr Linton will be home from church soon," I said. Heathcliff groaned, but Catherine was quiet and never moved.

Suddenly, I saw the servants and Mr Linton walking towards Thrushcross Grange. "He is here now!" I shouted. "Please go. Go out of the back door. You won't meet anyone if you go that way."

"I must go, Catherine," said Heathcliff, and he tried

to pull himself away from her. "But I will be under your window all night. I will not leave you."

"You must not go!" she answered, and she held him against her. "You *shall* not! I will die, Heathcliff, I will die!" Then her head fell back, and her arms dropped to the floor.

At that moment, Mr Linton entered the room. When he saw Heathcliff, Mr Linton's face was very angry, but he quickly took his wife in his arms. "I will go," Heathcliff said, "but I will stay in the garden under the trees. Nelly, please bring me news of her, or I will come back. I don't care if Linton is here or not!"

At midnight, Cathy, who you met at Wuthering Heights, was born. She was very small and was born two months early. Two hours after that, her mother died. Edgar was filled with grief, and he was always a sad man after that. He was sad because of Catherine's death, of course, but also because Cathy was a daughter, not a son.

"Cathy will have no control over her life when she gets married," Edgar thought, sadly. "When I die, the house and her money will belong to her husband. So, a man will always own Thrushcross Grange."

The following morning was sunny. Mr Linton lay quietly next to his wife's body. I went outside quietly and found Mr Heathcliff standing under the trees in the gardens with his hat in his hand. As I walked towards him, he lifted his dark eyes and looked at me. "She's dead," he said. "I've not waited here for hours for you to tell me that. Don't cry, Nelly – she doesn't want you to cry!"

But I was crying for him, too. "Yes, she is dead," I replied. "And did she ever say my name?"

"She did not wake up again after you left her," I replied. "Now, she lies with a sweet smile on her face. I hope she wakes happily in heaven."

He hit his head against the tree then and growled like a wild animal. When he looked up, he had blood on his face. Then, he kicked the ground hard with his foot. "I cannot live without my life!" he screamed. "I cannot live without my soul!"

Catherine Linton's funeral was on the Friday after her death. Hindley did not come, and Isabella was not asked to come. Catherine was **buried** near a low wall next to the moor that she loved.

CHAPTER EIGHT
Isabella escapes

After Catherine's death, the early spring weather changed again. The sky turned grey, snow came and the birds went silent. Mr Linton stayed in his room, and I looked after Cathy in one of the downstairs rooms. One morning, three days after Catherine's funeral, I was sitting with Cathy on my knee when the door opened. A woman entered, breathing hard and laughing.

"I'm sorry," she said, "but I know that Edgar is in bed, and I could not stop myself. I have run here from Wuthering Heights!"

It was Isabella. Her blonde hair had fallen wildly around her shoulders, and her thin clothes were wet with snow. One of her eyes was bruised, and she had a cut under one ear. I made her change her clothes, then sat her in front of the fire with a cup of tea.

"Sit down, Nelly," she said. "And put the baby down. I'm so sorry about Catherine – but I am not sorry for Heathcliff. That awful man has killed my heart! How could Catherine be his friend?" Then, she took off her wedding ring and threw it into the fire. "A carriage is coming to take me to London. Of course, I would like to stay here because I can help Edgar, and it is my home. But Heathcliff will hate that. He won't want me to be comfortable and happy, so he will come here to get revenge on me."

"Tell me what happened at Wuthering Heights," I said.

"Hindley wanted to go to the funeral," she replied. "So he was trying not to drink much the night before, but this meant he was even more angry and unhappy than usual. He and I were sitting by the fire, and we heard Heathcliff come home. It was the first time we had seen him for more than a week. Hindley suddenly got up with a knife. 'You and I both hate that man,' he said, 'and now I am going to kill him.'

"Heathcliff came into the kitchen, and Hindley ran at him, but Heathcliff hit Hindley, and the knife fell to the floor. Then, he picked up a big stone and hit Hindley with it! Hindley fell down, bleeding from his nose. Then, Heathcliff kicked him and hit his head again and again against the stone floor.

"After that, he hit me, too, and threw me on the floor next to Hindley. 'Get out of here,' he said. At that moment, Joseph came, and I got up and ran to my room. I stayed a few more days, but Heathcliff was mad with grief because of Catherine's death, and he kept shouting at me and hitting me. Finally, I woke up early this morning and collected my things. Then, I came straight here."

Soon after, a carriage came and took Isabella to London. A few months later, she gave birth to a son called Linton, who she described in her letters as a "thin and weak" child. She never returned to Thrushcross Grange, but later she and her brother began writing to each other.

Six months after Catherine's death, the doctor from

Gimmerton told me that Mr Hindley had also died — because of his drinking. I immediately went to Mr Linton.

"Hareton is your nephew, so he should come to live with us," I said. "There is nothing for him at Wuthering Heights." Mr Linton was not sure, but he finally agreed to let me go to Wuthering Heights. He told me that Hindley had owed Heathcliff a lot of money because of losing card games. "Wuthering Heights is Mr Heathcliff's now," he said. "Hindley gave it to Heathcliff to pay him the money that he owed. Hareton is poor — he does not own Wuthering Heights, and he has no money."

But, when I got to Wuthering Heights, Mr Heathcliff would not let me take Hareton. "I want to keep a child here," he said. "So, if you take Hareton, I will ask Isabella for my child."

When I got back, I repeated Mr Heathcliff's words to Mr Linton. He was worried that, if we asked for his nephew, Heathcliff would ask Isabella for Linton. This stopped us from asking for Hareton again.

CHAPTER NINE
Little Cathy

The twelve years that followed Catherine's death were the happiest of my life. Little Cathy grew quickly, and she could walk and talk before she was two. She was beautiful, with the Earnshaws' dark eyes but the Lintons' pale skin and gold hair. She could be naughty, but she was never spoiled or wild like her mother, and she had a warm, loving heart.

She was very close to her father, and, until she was thirteen, she never went out of the gardens alone. She did not know about Wuthering Heights or Mr Heathcliff. She seemed happy at Thrushcross Grange, but sometimes she looked out of the window at the moor and said, "Nelly, how long will it be before I can walk out on the moor? What is on the other side of those hills? Is it the sea?"

"No, Miss Cathy," I replied. "There are more hills. Just like these."

"And why do those rocks look like gold in the evening?" she asked.

"They are the Penistone Crags. They are gold because they are high, so the sun touches them late in the evening," I said. "In winter, there is always snow there before it snows here. Sometimes, snow lies there in summer, too!"

"Oh, you have visited them. Then I can visit them, too, when I am a woman."

"Your father will tell you that they are not very exciting," I replied. I knew that she had to pass Wuthering Heights to visit Penistone Crags, and I did not want her to go to that house. "The moor and the gardens are much nicer. Thrushcross Grange is the nicest place in the world."

"But I know the gardens, and I don't know that place," she said, quietly. "I would love to ride my pony to Penistone Crags sometime."

In July, twelve years after leaving her husband, Isabella died, although I do not know what her illness was. When he heard the news, Mr Linton went away for three weeks. He planned to bring Linton home with him. At first, Cathy was too unhappy to read or play, so I started making her go into the gardens. Sometimes, she walked with Charlie, one of Mr Linton's dogs, and sometimes she went out on a pony.

It was a beautiful summer. Sometimes, she stayed outside from breakfast until tea. But, one day, the naughty girl did not come home. Then, one of the servants told me that she had seen Cathy riding her pony towards Penistone Crags.

"What will happen to her?" I shouted. I followed the road to Wuthering Heights. There, I saw Charlie, Mr Linton's dog, lying under a window with blood on his face.

The housekeeper, Zillah, opened the door. She was from Gimmerton and had worked at Wuthering Heights since Hindley died. "Are you looking for Miss Cathy?" she asked me. "Don't worry, she is safe here, but I'm happy that Mr Heathcliff and Joseph are away."

I entered and saw Cathy in a little chair. She was laughing and talking to Hareton. He was now a strong, handsome young man of eighteen, but he wore the clothes of a farm worker, and his hair was wild. He was watching her with huge interest and surprise.

"Nelly!" she cried. "I have a wonderful story to tell you."

"Miss Cathy, put your hat on and come home now!" I said. "You cannot go riding again before your father gets back. He will not be happy about this!"

"But Nelly, what have I done?" she cried.

"Miss Cathy, you do not know who owns this house."

Cathy turned to Hareton. "Your father owns it, doesn't he?"

"No," he replied, and he turned away.

"Whose house is it then? A minute ago you were talking about 'our house' and 'our family'. Are you a servant? If you are a servant, you should call me 'Miss'."

Hareton's face became very angry. "I will never be your servant. I'd prefer to kill you!" he said.

"You'd *what*?" she replied, her face shocked.

"You rude girl!" he said.

"Come, Miss Cathy!" I cried. "Let's go."

"But Nelly, how can he speak to me like that?" she cried. "You awful boy – I will tell my father about you!"

Hareton did not seem worried about Edgar Linton, and suddenly Cathy looked like she was going to cry.

"Miss Cathy, Hareton is not your servant, he is your *cousin*," I said.

"My cousin?" she shouted, then laughed loudly. "You are not my cousin. My father has gone to get my cousin, Linton, from London."

"Shh, Miss Cathy," I said, quickly, because I did not want Mr Heathcliff to know that Linton was coming to Thrushcross Grange.

We called Joseph and asked for the pony and Charlie, and we left Wuthering Heights quickly. Cathy told me that Hareton's dogs had attacked hers as she rode past Wuthering Heights on her way to Penistone Crags.

I made her promise not to tell her father about the visit. At first, she was unhappy about this, but then she agreed.

A week after our visit to Wuthering Heights, a letter came from Edgar Linton. It said that he was returning soon with Isabella's son and asked me to get a room ready for him.

Cathy was wild with excitement when she heard about her cousin. "Linton is just six months younger than I am," she said a few days later, as we waited for them in the garden on a beautiful hot day. "He is going to be my friend! Oh, I'm so happy!"

When the carriage finally arrived, Cathy shouted as she saw her father's face in the window. He got out of the carriage quickly and threw his arms around her. I went past them and looked in the carriage. Linton was asleep in the corner with a coat around him. He was weak and pale, with gold hair. He looked very like Mr Linton, but he was much thinner and weaker.

The boy was very tired from the journey, and when I woke him up he began to cry. He came into the house and lay down quietly on a sofa as I went to get some tea. When I came back, Cathy was sitting next to him, and she was touching his hair and kissing his cheek. This seemed to make him happy, and he stopped crying and smiled.

"He will be fine," said Mr Linton.

"If we can keep him," I replied, quietly.

I was right to be afraid. The next morning, Joseph came to the door. "Heathcliff has sent me for his boy," he said to Mr Linton. "And I mustn't go home without him."

51

Mr Linton was quiet for a moment, his face worried. But there was nothing that he could do. Linton was Heathcliff's son, and Mr Linton did not have the power to stop Linton's father from taking him. "Tell Mr Heathcliff that his son shall come to Wuthering Heights tomorrow. He is in bed and is too tired to travel now."

"No," said Joseph. "Mr Heathcliff wants him tonight."

"Not tonight!" answered Mr Linton, and he turned and closed the door.

"Tomorrow, then!" shouted Joseph, and he slowly walked away. "Tomorrow, or Mr Heathcliff will come himself to take him."

CHAPTER TEN
A walk on the moor

Joseph came for Linton early the next morning, and Cathy was very sad and confused when she woke up to find her cousin was not there. I told her he had gone to live with another family who lived many miles away. After that, she sometimes asked questions about him, but then she slowly forgot him.

Three years passed, until she was sixteen. Her birthday was not a happy day for her father, because it was also the day of her mother's death, and he always spent it alone in the library. This meant Cathy was alone, too. But, this year, it was a beautiful March day, and Cathy came down dressed for a walk on the moor. Mr Linton was happy for her to go with me, but we had to be back in an hour.

"Quickly, Nelly," Cathy said as we left Thrushcross Grange. "I want to see some birds in their nest. I know where they are."

I put on my hat and followed her on to the moor. She ran in front of me, and her eyes were bright and happy as her gold hair lifted in the spring wind.

But she walked and walked until I became tired and shouted to her to stop. But she was far ahead of me and did not hear, or did not want to hear. Then, she turned a corner in the road, and Wuthering Heights appeared. Suddenly, two people were standing next to her. One of them was Hareton, and the other was Mr Heathcliff. He was shouting at her.

"I haven't found or taken any birds," she was saying as I came up. "I just wanted to see the nest. Father told me about it."

Mr Heathcliff gave me a strange smile, then turned back to her. "And who is 'Father'?" he asked.

"Mr Linton from Thrushcross Grange. And who are you?" she replied. Then she pointed to Hareton. "I've met this boy before. Is he your son?"

"Miss Cathy," I said, quickly, "we've been out for three hours. We must go back."

"No, that man is not my son," answered Heathcliff, pushing me to one side. "But I've got a son, and you've met him. Why don't you come to my house for a rest? He will be happy to see you."

"Do not say yes!" I whispered into her ear. "You must not!"

"Why not?" Cathy asked, loudly. "I'm tired, and I want to see his son. Does he live at the big house I visited when I went to Penistone Crags?"

"He does," replied Mr Heathcliff. "Now be quiet, Nelly. It will be nice for her to come to Wuthering Heights and see my son. Hareton, take the girl with you. I will walk with Nelly."

I argued with Mr Heathcliff as we followed the pair towards the house, but he kept telling me to be quiet. Then he opened the door and invited Cathy in with a smile. Was he being kind to her because she was Catherine's daughter?

Did she make him think of Catherine? I wasn't sure.

Linton stood near the fire. He was still thin, but he had grown a bit taller and was now quite handsome. His eyes were brighter, and his face was not as pale as it had been when he arrived at Thrushcross Grange. But maybe he looked healthier because of the spring air.

"Linton!" cried Cathy. "Is that Linton? He is taller than I am now."

The boy moved forward and said hello. She kissed him excitedly, and they stared at each other in surprise because they had both changed a lot. After they had talked to each other for a few minutes, she turned to Heathcliff. "You are my uncle," she said. "I like you, although you were angry at the beginning. Why haven't you visited Thrushcross Grange with Linton?"

"I came before once or twice – and often before you were born," replied Mr Heathcliff. "But Mr Linton does not like me. If you tell him about this visit, he will stop you coming here."

We stayed all afternoon. I could not make Cathy leave sooner. She and Linton were laughing at Hareton because he could not read. But Hareton quickly grew angry and shouted back at them.

Finally, she agreed to come with me if she could visit Linton the next day. But as soon as we got home, she told her father about her meeting with Linton and Mr Heathcliff. Mr Linton was very unhappy. "You must not go there again," he said. "Mr Heathcliff is an awful man."

"But he was nice to me, Father. Why did Nelly tell me that Linton lived many miles away?"

"Because we didn't want you to visit Wuthering Heights, Cathy," Mr Linton replied. "Mr Heathcliff hates me, and he was very unkind to your aunt, Isabella. This is why I didn't want you to visit Linton – because I did not want you to see Mr Heathcliff. When you are older, you will understand everything."

Cathy was quiet after that, but in the evening I found her in her room. She was on her knees, and she was crying.

"Oh, Nelly, I'm not crying for myself. I'm crying for Linton," she said. "He thinks that I am coming to see him tomorrow, and he will be very unhappy."

"Don't be stupid," I said. "He has Hareton as a friend. He does not need you."

"But please can I write him a small note to explain?"

"No, you can't."

"Please, Nelly . . ." and she gave me a very sweet look. But I said no again and left her. But, some weeks later, I was cleaning her bedroom, and I found a lot of letters. She and Linton were writing words of love to each other daily. I immediately threw the letters in the fire and sent a note to Wuthering Heights: *Linton Heathcliff must not send any more letters to Miss Cathy*.

Later, Cathy told me that a boy from the village had taken the notes to Wuthering Heights for her. She was very angry at me, and sad, of course, but after I sent my note the letters stopped.

Autumn came. Dry, red leaves lay on the ground, and clouds covered the cold blue sky. Mr Linton and Cathy went for long walks in the fields and often did not come home until late evening. Then, Mr Linton was ill, and he had to stay in bed. Cathy had become quieter and sadder after the letters to Linton stopped, and now she was **lonely** without her father. I tried to be with her as much as possible, but then I was also ill for a short time.

I had to stay in bed, too, and Cathy was wonderful. She came back and forward from Mr Linton's room to mine and shared her time between us. But Mr Linton usually went to bed early, and I did not need much after 6 p.m., so I did not know what she did with her evenings.

One evening, after three weeks in bed, I was finally able to leave my bedroom. I was walking around the house, which seemed strangely quiet, when Cathy suddenly climbed in through one of the windows in the sitting room. In the garden, I could see a boy walking away with her pony.

"Miss Cathy!" I cried. "Where have you been?"

"Just around the gardens," she replied, but her face went very red.

"Oh, Cathy," I said, "please don't lie to me."

She began to cry then, and she put her arms around my neck. "Oh, Nelly, please don't be angry. I have been to Wuthering Heights. Mr Heathcliff came here when you were ill. 'Linton is so unhappy, he is lonely without you,' he said. I've been to see him every day since you became ill. I've not been happy about it. Wuthering Heights is so cold in this autumn weather, and we have only had three or four happy days together there. But Linton is not well, and he's so happy when I visit. Sometimes, I think he will die. Linton can sometimes be a spoiled little boy, but his father shouts at him and says horrible things about his weak body, and Hareton is stupid and cannot read."

"Hush!" I said. "Hareton is your cousin as much as Linton. You must not speak about him like that."

"Please don't stop me going to Wuthering Heights, Nelly. I know that Linton is a weak and sad boy, but if I don't go he will be so unhappy. Please don't tell Father."

"I will think about that, Miss Cathy. Now, go to bed."

But I went straight from my bedroom to her father's and told him everything. Mr Linton was very worried, and the next morning he told her that she had to stop visiting her cousin. Cathy cried and asked him again and again to think about Linton.

Winter passed and spring came, but Mr Linton's health did not get better. Cathy continued to worry about her cousin Linton, and, finally, Mr Linton wrote to invite him to Thrushcross Grange. A few days later, he got a reply. Mr Heathcliff did not want Linton to visit Thrushcross Grange, but he was happy if he and Miss Cathy met on the moor. Mr Linton was, of course, too ill to go with Cathy. "You can write to Linton again," he said. "And perhaps, in the summer, I will allow you to meet him again."

CHAPTER ELEVEN
A terrible wedding

It was late August before Edgar finally allowed Cathy and me to meet Linton. We started out one morning on a warm, grey day. But we found Linton a long way from where we had agreed to meet him, and he was near Wuthering Heights. He was lying on the grass and did not lift his head until we came close.

Cathy looked at him with surprise and grief. "Your health is worse," she said.

"No, it's better . . . better!" he cried and took her hand. "I'm just tired. It is too hot."

The two spoke for some minutes, but Linton did not seem interested in the conversation, and he kept looking nervously at Wuthering Heights. He seemed frightened of something and was not always listening to his cousin.

"What is making him so nervous?" I thought.

"I think that you must go home," Cathy said, finally. "You will be more comfortable there, and I cannot make you laugh today."

They agreed to meet again in a week's time. But, during that week, Mr Linton's illness suddenly got much worse, and Cathy did not want to leave him. She spent all her time with her father, helping him to sit or just sitting next to him. Finally, Mr Linton made her go to meet her cousin, because he wanted her to be outside and happy.

Linton was lying on the grass at the same place where we had met him before, but as we reached him he turned towards Wuthering Heights with a frightened look. Then we saw Mr Heathcliff coming over the hill. He did not look at Linton or Cathy, but straight at me.

"Is it true, Nelly?" he asked. "Is Edgar Linton dying?"

"Yes, he is dying," I replied, "and I don't know how long he will live."

"I'm asking this question because my son is going to die before me," Heathcliff said, "and I would like his uncle to die before him."

"Your son should not be here, Mr Heathcliff. He should be in bed, and a doctor should see him."

"He will be in a day or two," replied Mr Heathcliff, and then he turned to Linton. "Get up, boy!"

Linton's face was pale and frightened.

"Take my hand!" shouted Mr Heathcliff. "Miss Linton, give him your arm. Please help me get him home."

"But I can't go to Wuthering Heights," Cathy whispered. "Father said that I mustn't."

But Linton took Cathy's hand and cried and **begged** her to come with them. I could not stop her, and how could I say no? We did not know what was making him so frightened and unhappy, but we did not want to make him worse. Cathy walked into the kitchen and made Linton sit in a chair next to the dresser. Then, Mr Heathcliff pushed me forward, locked the door behind me and took the key.

"You will have tea before you go," he said. "Zillah, Hareton and Joseph are out tonight, and I am alone. Miss Cathy, I'm going to give you a present. I know it's not a good present, but it's all I have to give you. Why are you staring at me like that?"

Cathy moved towards him, her eyes bright and angry. "I am not frightened of you," she said. "Give me that key. I will have it!"

"If you don't step back, I will hit you!" he shouted.

But she caught his hand and tried to pull his fingers away from the key. Heathcliff took her hair, then hit her repeatedly around the head.

When I saw him do this, I ran at him. "Stop it, stop it!" I shouted, but he hit me, too, so that I couldn't breathe properly. I fell back to the floor, as Cathy put her hands to her head and began to shake. Then, she began to cry.

"Father wants Cathy and me to be married," said Linton, quietly. "He's worried that I might die if we wait. So, we must get married in the morning. After you do this, you can go home and take me with you."

"Marry?" I replied, and I started to shake him hard. "Are you mad? Do you think a beautiful, healthy young girl like her will marry a weak thing like you?"

Linton started to groan and then to cry. "Please, Cathy, save me," he begged. "Let me come to Thrushcross Grange with you. You must say yes to my father – you *must*!"

"What can I do?" asked Cathy. "If I stay, Father will be worried and unhappy. He will think that I have betrayed him. Mr Heathcliff, let me go home. I promise I will marry Linton."

"Good!" said Mr Heathcliff. "I want your father to be unhappy. And you will keep your promise, because I will not allow you to leave this place until you have married Linton."

"Send Nelly, then!" begged Cathy. "She can let Father know that I am safe. Or marry me now. Oh, Nelly, what shall we do?"

Miss Cathy and Linton were married the next morning,

but Mr Heathcliff betrayed us and kept us locked in at Wuthering Heights for five days. On the sixth morning, he let me go, and I ran across the moor to Thrushcross Grange to get help. Poor Mr Linton was now very ill and waiting for his death. He lay in bed with his eyes closed, whispering Cathy's name.

Then, soon after, Cathy appeared and threw her arms around my neck, crying, "Nelly! Nelly! Is Father still alive?"

"Yes!" I said. "Yes, he is. Thank God you are safe again."

I watched her run to her father's room, but I didn't go in with her. Instead, I waited outside quietly while they spent their last hours together. She put her arms around him, and he looked into her eyes. Then, he whispered, "I am going to your mother, my child, and you will come to us." He didn't speak again after that, and, a little later, he died.

The evening after the funeral, we spoke about the future. Maybe Cathy could live at Thrushcross Grange with Linton, and I could stay with them as housekeeper. I knew that I was hoping for a lot, but it was possible.

Suddenly, a servant came running into the room and shouted, "Mr Heathcliff is here." Mr Heathcliff did not knock on the door, but came straight in. Cathy rose from her chair and started to run, but he caught her arm and shouted, "Stop! I've come to take you home. I need you there to look after my son."

"Please," I said. "Why don't you let them live here? You don't like them and won't miss them."

"I want a tenant for Thrushcross Grange," he replied.

"And I want to have my children with me. Get ready now, and don't make me wait."

Cathy went upstairs and left me alone with Mr Heathcliff. "If I can't stay here, then let me come to Wuthering Heights," I said. "Let me have Zillah's job."

But he would not agree. Then, he started to walk around the room, looking at the pictures until he came to one of Cathy's mother. "I will have that," he said, and he took it down. Then, he turned and said with a strange smile, "I'll tell you what I did last night, Nelly. I went to her grave and took away the earth. Then, I opened the coffin. I wanted to see her face again!"

"You are a terrible man, Mr Heathcliff. You must not **disturb** the dead," I said.

"I disturbed nobody," he replied. "But her ghost has disturbed me, night and day, for eighteen years."

Mr Heathcliff stopped speaking and put his hand to his face. Then, Cathy came back and said that she was ready.

"Goodbye, Nelly," she whispered, and she kissed me. "Please come and see me. Don't forget."

"She will not come and see you!" shouted Mr Heathcliff to Cathy. "I do not want Nelly coming to my house and talking about us to other people." Then, he turned to me. "If I want to see you, Nelly, then I will come here."

CHAPTER TWELVE
The note

I visited Wuthering Heights once after Cathy left, but Joseph held the door closed and would not let me enter. Now, I get my news from Zillah, who thinks that Cathy is proud and does not like her. The first thing Cathy did when she arrived was to run upstairs and lock herself in Linton's room, Zillah told me. The next day, she came down and asked for the doctor. She said that Linton was very ill and needed medicine.

"We know that," replied Mr Heathcliff. "But Linton's life is worth nothing, so I will spend nothing on him."

After that, Cathy stayed with Linton. He cried and groaned, and she could not sleep No one would help her or send for the doctor.

One night in late September, about a month after she had married Linton, Cathy went to Zillah. "Tell Mr Heathcliff that his son is dying," she said.

Zillah took Cathy's message to Mr Heathcliff. A few minutes later, he came out with a lantern and went to Linton's room. Zillah followed. Cathy was sitting next to the bed. Heathcliff held up the lantern and looked at his son. "Well, he is dead," he said. Then he turned to her. "Now, Cathy, how do you feel?"

She was quiet.

"How do you feel?" he repeated.

"He's safe, and I am free," she answered. "So, I should feel well. But I have been with him so many hours alone that I feel like I am dead myself!"

After Linton's death, Cathy stayed upstairs for two weeks. Zillah tried to help her, but she proudly asked to be left alone. Mr Heathcliff went up once to show her Linton's **will**. Because Mr Heathcliff had made her marry Linton, and then Edgar Linton had died, Heathcliff's son had owned Thrushcross Grange. Now Linton was dead, and he had left everything to his father in his will.

Mr Heathcliff now owned Wuthering Heights and Thrushcross Grange. Cathy was left with nothing, and she had nowhere to go. This is why she has to live at Wuthering Heights and is so unhappy. Linton died last winter, sir.

―――――

When Nelly had finished the story, she said, "Only a year ago! I did not believe that one year later I would be telling this story to a stranger. But I can see that you like Cathy Linton, sir. And you cannot be happy living alone . . ."

"Stop!" I said, and I laughed. "Yes, I may love her. But why would she love me? And I live in the city and must return there. No, Mrs Dean, it is not possible . . ."

After I had listened to Nelly Dean's story, I decided that I had to leave Thrushcross Grange as soon as possible. I did not want to live near to my landlord for one more second. I am now much better and, although it is the middle of January, I have decided to ride to Wuthering Heights to let Mr Heathcliff know that I am leaving. I came to Thrushcross Grange in October and have rented it for one year. I plan to spend the next six months in London, and he can look for another tenant after October. I will not spend another winter in this place.

Yesterday was a bright and cold January morning. I rode to Wuthering Heights and took a note from Nelly Dean to Cathy. When I got there, the front door was open but the gate was locked. I saw Hareton in the garden and called him. He came and opened it.

We entered the house together. Cathy was sitting in front of the fire, cutting vegetables for lunch. She was quieter than before, and her beautiful face was very unhappy. She looked at me quickly, but she did not say hello. I moved towards her and quietly put Nelly's note next to her hand. She looked at it quickly and then at me. "What is this?" she asked, loudly, and pushed it on to the floor.

"It's a note from Mrs Dean," I said.

Hareton immediately ran across the kitchen and took it before she could pick it back up. "Mr Heathcliff should see this first!" he said.

Cathy turned away from us and began to cry. Hareton stared at her for a few seconds, and then he threw the note at the floor by her feet. She took it quickly and read it.

"Oh, I want to be at Thrushcross Grange!" she said. "Oh, I'm tired, Hareton!" And she threw her head back and closed her eyes.

"Mrs Heathcliff," I said. "Nelly is always talking about you. Please can you give me some news to take to her?"

"You must tell her," replied Cathy, "that I would like to answer her letter. But there is no paper in this house and no books."

"No books!" I cried. "How can you live without them?"

"Mr Heathcliff never reads," she said, "so he burned my books. I have not seen one for weeks. Once, Hareton, I found some books in your room. Some stories and poetry. I took them to read, but you stole them back – although they are no use to you because you can't read."

When he heard this, Hareton turned red. "I did not take those books!" he cried.

"I think Hareton would like to learn to read," I said, trying to help him. "He wants to be like you."

"And he will see me become stupid at the same time," she replied, tiredly, "because there is no one intelligent here to talk to."

At that moment, Heathcliff entered. He had changed since I last saw him. He looked thinner, and his face was more sad than angry.

Cathy immediately stood up and went to the kitchen. Hareton watched her go. Heathcliff did not see me, but looked at the two young people. Then, he said to himself quietly, "It is strange. But when I look for Hindley in his face, I see only hers. It is difficult to look at him."

I stepped forward then and told him that I was there.

"It's good to see you out of your house, Mr Lockwood," Mr Heathcliff replied. "I was worried that you were unhappy here in this wild place."

"It was a stupid idea to live here," I said. "I must go back to London next week, and I will not keep Thrushcross Grange after October."

"Well, you must pay for the full twelve months for the **tenancy**," he replied. "Mr Lockwood, you must stay for dinner. Cathy! Bring the things in. Where are you?"

Cathy quickly appeared with some knives and forks. "Have your dinner with Joseph," he said to her, "and stay in the kitchen until Mr Lockwood has gone."

She left immediately. She was beautiful, and I liked her, but she did not seem to like me. I thought that maybe she did not meet many gentlemen.

With Mr Heathcliff on one side and Hareton on the other, it was a quiet, unhappy meal. When it was finished, I got up and said goodbye quickly. I was hoping to see Cathy one more time on my way out, but Hareton took me to my horse, so it was not possible.

"How boring life must be in that house!" I thought, as I rode towards Thrushcross Grange. "It would be so different if Cathy and I were friends, and I could take her away to London!"

CHAPTER THIRTEEN
Mr Lockwood returns

1802 – In September of that same year, I was invited to visit a friend in Yorkshire, and on my way to his home I found myself close to Gimmerton. I suddenly decided that I wanted to go to Thrushcross Grange. I could stay in my own bed instead of a **guest-house** and visit Mr Heathcliff to discuss the rent money for Thrushcross Grange.

When I got to Thrushcross Grange, it was evening. I knocked on the door but nobody answered, so I rode around the house and found an old woman sitting on the steps.

"Is Nelly Dean inside?" I asked.

"Nelly?" she replied. "No. She's at Wuthering Heights."

"Are you the housekeeper here, then?"

"I look after the house," she replied.

"Well, I am the tenant, Mr Lockwood."

She stood up quickly. "Mr Lockwood!" she cried. "Why didn't you tell us that you were coming? The house isn't ready."

I told her that I only wanted a clean bed, food and a good fire. There was no need to clean the house for me.

"Is everything all right at Wuthering Heights?" I asked, following her inside.

"I think so," she said, putting wood on the fire.

I wanted to ask why Nelly Dean had left Thrushcross Grange, but the housekeeper was too busy getting things ready. So I started walking across the moor towards Wuthering Heights. It was night, but the moon was full and bright. When I got there, the gate was open, and the smell of autumn flowers came to me from the garden.

"This is different," I thought.

The front door was open, too, and I could see and hear the people inside talking.

"*Diff-ic-ult!*" said a sweet voice. "This is the third time, you stupid boy. I'm not going to say it again."

"Difficult, then," said another, deeper voice. "And now kiss me for saying it so well."

The second voice was that of a handsome young man. He was dressed in nice clothes and sitting at a table with a book in front of him. His face was happy, and his eyes kept moving from the page to a small white hand on his shoulder. Cathy stood behind him, her gold hair sometimes meeting his dark hair as she put her head down to read his writing. She was smiling. I suddenly felt angry with myself. Why hadn't I tried harder to make her love me? But it was too late now.

Hareton read the word again, and suddenly Cathy gave him five quick kisses. Then, they came to the door and began to walk happily together out on to the moor. I did not want them to see me, so I walked around the outside of the house and found that the kitchen door was also open. Nelly Dean was sitting inside.

"Why, it's Mr Lockwood," said Nelly, when I entered. "Why didn't you tell us that you were coming?"

"I'm only staying for one night," I replied. "I'm leaving tomorrow. So, why are you here, Nelly? Tell me."

"Zillah left," she replied. "Mr Heathcliff asked me to stay here until you returned from London and needed me at Thrushcross Grange. Have you come from Gimmerton?"

"From Thrushcross Grange," I said, sitting down in a chair opposite her. "I wanted to talk to Mr Heathcliff about the rent while I was here."

"Oh, then you must talk to me, or Miss Cathy," she said. "But she's gone out with Hareton now. Ah, but you haven't heard that Mr Heathcliff is dead, have you?"

"Heathcliff *dead*!" I said, shocked. "How long ago?"

"Three months ago," she replied. Then, she told me the end of her story.

———

A fortnight after you left us, Mr Heathcliff asked me to come back to Wuthering Heights. Of course, I was happy to be back with Miss Cathy again. But, when I got here, I was shocked. She had changed so much. Mr Heathcliff told me that he was tired of seeing her, and I had to live in one of the rooms and keep her with me. She was happy about this, and I slowly brought her books and other things from Thrushcross Grange.

But soon she grew bored and lonely. She preferred to go to the kitchen to argue with Joseph than stay in our small room. Hareton often went there, too, and he was always silent and angry. She was rude to him at first and told him he was stupid and lazy. "How can he spend a whole evening sleeping in front of the fire?" she said. Then, she laughed. "He's like a dog, isn't he, Nelly? Or a horse. He works, eats and sleeps. How boring!"

"Mr Hareton will ask Mr Heathcliff to send you upstairs if you don't stop speaking to him like this," I replied, seeing Hareton move his hand.

"I know why Hareton never speaks to me," she went on. "He thinks that I will laugh at him. He began to teach himself to read once, and, because I laughed, he burned his books. That was stupid, wasn't it, Hareton?"

She went upstairs. In the morning, I knew that she was sorry for teasing him. But she was clever, and after that she started reading out loud when Hareton was in the kitchen. Then, she would put the book down at an interesting part and leave it near him. But he never picked it up.

One Monday, Joseph took some cows to Gimmerton. Hareton was in the kitchen, and Cathy kept looking at her cousin, but he would not look at her. Finally, she turned, and I heard her say, "Hareton. I would like you to be my cousin now. Please don't be so angry and rough with me. I don't think that you're stupid. I like you."

Hareton did not answer.

"You should be friends with your cousin, Hareton," I said. "If you were, then you would be a much happier man."

"A friend!" he shouted. "But she hates me and thinks she is better than me."

"I don't hate you. You hate me!" Cathy cried. "I was unhappy before, and angry. Please forgive me. What more can I say?"

She took one of her books and covered it in paper, and she wrote "Mr Hareton Earnshaw" on it. Then, she asked me to take it to him. "Tell him that, if he takes it, I will teach him to read," she said.

I took the book to him and put it gently on his knee. He did not pick it up, but he did not throw it off, either. I went back to my work.

A little later, I came back into the room and saw their two

heads together over the book. Their eyes were bright, and they were both smiling.

That next morning, we had breakfast with Mr Heathcliff. Cathy was putting small flowers in Hareton's food, and he was trying not to laugh. Then he *did* laugh. Mr Heathcliff lifted his head quickly in surprise, but Cathy looked back at him with proud, angry eyes. "It's a good thing I can't reach you from here!" he shouted. "Why do you look back at me with your mother's eyes? Stop it! I thought that I had stopped you from laughing."

"It was me who laughed," said Hareton, quietly.

"What did you say?" shouted Mr Heathcliff.

Hareton looked down and said nothing more, but Heathcliff immediately turned to Cathy. "Are you trying to make him hate me?" he cried. "Get away, do you hear. Hareton, make her go!"

"He won't listen to you now," said Cathy. "And soon he'll hate you as much as I do. You have taken my house and my

money. You have taken Hareton's house and money, too. We are friends now, and I shall tell him all about you!"

Heathcliff immediately reached out and took her hair. As Hareton moved to stop him, Heathcliff's eyes were very angry, and I knew that he was planning to hit her. Then, suddenly, his hand moved to her arm, and he stared hard into her face. "You must stop making me angry, or I will murder you one day," he said, suddenly, in a softer voice. "Nelly, take her and leave me, all of you! Leave me!"

A little later, he went out, and he said that he would not come back until the evening.

CHAPTER FOURTEEN
Young love

While he was gone, Cathy and Hareton sat together and continued with their reading lesson. It was wonderful to watch them together. Don't forget that they were both my children, and I was proud of them. With Cathy's help, Hareton has changed into a warm and intelligent young gentleman.

When I was with them it was easy to forget time, and, when Mr Heathcliff came in late and saw us all together, we did not hear him at first. The light from the fire shone on their beautiful young heads as they lifted their eyes together to look at him. Have you noticed how their eyes are the same? They are Catherine Earnshaw's eyes. But Hareton looks much more like her than Cathy.

He made them both leave, and then he turned to me. "It's a strange ending, isn't it?" he said. "I could hit them, but why? I don't care, Nelly. I don't enjoy hurting them now. Nelly, a change is happening. I'm not interested in my life. I forget to eat or drink. I won't speak about Cathy, and I don't want to think about her. But Hareton affects me differently.

"I see Catherine everywhere, Nelly. I see her in every cloud and in every tree. Everything in the world tells me that she lived, and I have lost her. Hareton looks like Catherine, and that is why I prefer not to see him."

"But what do you mean by a 'change', Mr Heathcliff?" I asked. "Are you ill?"

"No," he replied. "With my strong body, I know I can live for many years. But I don't want to, Nelly. I have to tell myself to breathe. I only want one thing, and everything is moving that way. I'm sure that it will happen soon. Oh God, it has been a long fight. I want it to be finished!"

After that evening, Mr Heathcliff stopped having meals with us, and he started to spend a lot of time outside. But it was strange, because when we saw him he did not seem unhappy. He seemed bright and excited, like something good was going to happen.

One evening, I heard him go downstairs and out of the front door. I did not hear him come back, and the next morning he was still away. The next day and the next evening he still did not return. When I woke up, it was raining. I walked around the house and saw that his bedroom window was open. "He cannot be in bed," I thought. "He must be downstairs or outside."

But when I opened the door to his bedroom, he was lying there on his back. His dark eyes met mine, and at first I did not think he was dead. But then I saw that his face and clothes were wet from the rain. When I put my fingers on his cold skin, I knew that he was dead.

We buried him next to Catherine's body. She lies now with Mr Linton on one side and Mr Heathcliff on the other. Hareton cried as he dropped the earth over his grave. Heathcliff had been like a father to him, and he could not see that Heathcliff had also been a terrible man.

I hope that Mr Heathcliff rests quietly in his grave, but once I was walking to Thrushcross Grange one evening, and I met a boy with some sheep. He was crying and shaking.

"What's the matter?" I asked him.

"Heathcliff and a woman are on the moor!" he cried. "I was too frightened to pass them."

I couldn't see anything, but neither the boy nor the sheep would go forward. I don't like walking on the moor at night now.

———

After that, Nelly went silent.

"So, who will live here now?" I asked.

"Only Joseph," she replied. "Hareton and Cathy will get married and go to Thrushcross Grange."

"Joseph and the ghosts," I said.

"No, Mr Lockwood," she replied, shaking her head. "I believe the dead sleep quietly."

I decided to visit the graves on my way home and found them easily near their low stone wall. I stood staring at them for a long time. The autumn sky above my head was kind, and a soft wind blew gently over the grass. And as I stood there I suddenly felt sure that Nelly was right – that these three people were sleeping quietly in that silent ground.

During-reading questions

Write the answers to these questions in your notebook.

CHAPTER ONE

1 Why does Mr Lockwood visit Wuthering Heights?
2 Why is Mr Lockwood excited about meeting Mr Heathcliff?
3 Why is the house called "Wuthering Heights"?

CHAPTER TWO

1 What sound wakes up Mr Lockwood?
2 What does Heathcliff do after he goes into Mr Lockwood's room?
3 How does Mr Lockwood get home?

CHAPTER THREE

1 Who is Nelly Dean, and how long has she worked at Thrushcross Grange? What other place has she worked?
2 Did Heathcliff have a daughter?
3 Who is Cathy's mother?
4 Who is Cathy's cousin?

CHAPTER FOUR

1 How does Heathcliff's life change after Hindley returns?
2 What do Catherine and Heathcliff do after Hindley returns?
3 What happens at Thrushcross Grange?
4 What does Mr Linton say to Hindley?
5 How has Catherine changed when she returns to Wuthering Heights?

CHAPTER FIVE

1 Why does Catherine think she can't marry Heathcliff?
2 Why does Heathcliff leave?
3 What does Catherine do after Heathcliff leaves?
4 Why is Edgar Linton the happiest man alive at the end of the chapter?

CHAPTER SIX

1 Who does Nelly meet in the garden when she is carrying apples?
2 How has this person changed?
3 What happens that makes Edgar Linton very angry?
4 What do Heathcliff and Isabella do at the end of the chapter?

CHAPTER SEVEN

1 Is Isabella happy living at Wuthering Heights? Why/Why not?
2 What happens when all the family except Catherine go to church?
3 Why is Edgar sad that Cathy is a girl?

CHAPTER EIGHT

1 Why does Isabella leave Wuthering Heights?
2 How does Hindley die?
3 Who owns Wuthering Heights now, and why?

CHAPTER NINE

1 Why doesn't Nelly want Cathy to go to Penistone Crags?
2 Why does Edgar go away for three weeks?
3 What happens to Cathy when she rides to Penistone Crags?
4 Why does Cathy want Hareton to call her "Miss"?

CHAPTER TEN

1 Why is Cathy's birthday not a happy day?
2 What does Cathy say she wants to see on the moor?
3 Why does Cathy go with Heathcliff to Wuthering Heights?
4 Why do Linton and Cathy laugh at Hareton?

CHAPTER ELEVEN

1 What does Heathcliff do when he returns to Wuthering
   Heights with Nelly, Cathy and Linton?
2 Why does Heathcliff want Cathy to marry Linton the
   next morning?
3 Why won't Heathcliff let Cathy and Linton live at
   Thrushcross Grange?
4 What did Heathcliff do at Catherine's grave, and why?

CHAPTER TWELVE

1 Heathcliff now owns Thrushcross Grange. Explain why.
2 Why does Mr Lockwood go back to Wuthering Heights?
3 "When I look for Hindley in his face, I see only hers,"
   Heathcliff says. What does he mean?

CHAPTER THIRTEEN

1 How do Cathy and Hareton become friends?
2 Why is Heathcliff angry at breakfast?
3 What does Heathcliff think Cathy is trying to do?

CHAPTER FOURTEEN

1 Why doesn't Heathcliff want to see Hareton?
2 How are things changing for Heathcliff?
3 Why was the boy with the sheep crying and shaking?

After-reading questions

1 How does Heathcliff change during the novel?
2 What kind of woman is Catherine Earnshaw? Describe her.
3 How is Cathy Linton different from her mother?
4 Heathcliff wants revenge on the Earnshaw and Linton families. Why does he want this revenge? Do you think he is right to want it?
5 "Oh God, it has been a long fight," Heathcliff says at the end of the story. Why does he say this, do you think?
6 Nelly tells the story of Wuthering Heights. How does she feel about the other people in the story?
7 Does *Wuthering Heights* have a happy ending, do you think? Why/Why not?
8 When Mr Lockwood comes to Wuthering Heights, he sees the date 1500 and the name "Hareton Earnshaw" written above the door. Why is this important?

Exercises

CHAPTER THREE

1 **Write the correct names in your notebook.**

1 ...*Mr Lockwood*.... is the tenant of Thrushcross Grange.

2 .... is the housekeeper at Thrushcross Grange.

3 .... is the daughter of Catherine Earnshaw.

4 .... is the husband of Catherine Earnshaw.

5 .... is Cathy's cousin.

6 .... is Hareton's father.

7 .... is Hindley's sister.

8 .... was found in Liverpool.

CHAPTER FOUR

2 **Make these sentences negative or positive in your notebook.**

1 He told us where Frances was from, probably because she had money.

   He never told us where Frances was from, probably because she .... *had no money* ....

2 Mr Hindley hadn't changed a lot.

3 He always saw Heathcliff and Catherine together and realized how rough and wild they were becoming.

4 "But we weren't laughing, and I don't think Mr and Mrs Linton heard us."

5 "Mr Hindley will be happy about this, Heathcliff," I said.

6 "She is not as beautiful as Isabella Linton, is she, Frances?"

CHAPTERS SIX AND SEVEN

3 **Write the correct words in your notebook.**

1 icmdiene ....*medicine*......... You have this when you are ill.

2 adrsc You use these to play a game, sometimes for money.

3 ebryat To behave badly towards someone who trusts you.

4 veneegr You sometimes want this when you are angry with someone.

5 racegrai A horse pulls this.

6 yubr When you put something under the ground.

CHAPTERS SEVEN AND EIGHT

4 **Who do you think is thinking this? Write the correct names in your notebook.**

| Edgar | Hindley | Catherine | Nelly | Isabella | Heathcliff |

1 "I know she is my sister, but I don't want to see her."
..........*Edgar*...........

2 "Everyone is at church. I will go to see her now."

3 "I think I am dying. I must kiss him one more time."

4 "I have to leave this house and these terrible men!"

5 "I am going to kill this man with this knife!"

6 "We must bring Hareton to Thrushcross Grange."

CHAPTER NINE

5 **Write the correct verbs in your notebook.**

1 "Sometimes, snow *lies* / **is lying** there in summer, too!"

2 "Oh, you **visited** / **have visited** them. Then I can **visit** / **visited** them, too, when I am a woman."

3 She was from Gimmerton and **worked** / **had worked** at Wuthering Heights **after** / **since** Hindley died.

4 "A minute ago you **were talking** / **talked** about 'our house' and 'our family'."

5 Hareton's dogs **were attacking** / **had attacked** hers as she rode past Wuthering Heights on her way to Penistone Crags.

6 "Heathcliff **has sent** / **sent** me for his boy."

CHAPTER TEN

6 **What happens here? Match the sentences to the answers in your notebook.**

Example: 1 – c

1 Cathy lives here.	**a**	the moor
2 Cathy meets Heathcliff and Hareton here.	**b**	Wuthering Heights
3 Cathy and her father walk here.	**c**	Thrushcross Grange
4 Cathy meets Linton here.	**d**	Cathy's room
5 Nelly finds letters here.	**e**	the fields

CHAPTER TWELVE

7 **Complete these sentences in your notebook, using the words or phrases from the box.**

> leave   tenant   landlord   look for   spend   decided

After I had listened to Nelly Dean's story, I decided that I had to ¹.......... *leave*.......... Thrushcross Grange as soon as possible. I did not want to live near to my ².......... for one more second. I am now much better and, although it is the middle of January, I have ³.......... to ride to Wuthering Heights to let Mr Heathcliff know that I am leaving. I came to Thrushcross Grange in October and have rented it for one year. I plan to ⁴.......... the next six months in London, and he can ⁵.......... another ⁶.......... after October. I will not spend another winter in this place.

CHAPTER THIRTEEN

8 **Write questions for these answers in your notebook.**

1 *Why did Lockwood go to Thrushcross Grange?*
   Because he was in Yorkshire.
2 Because the gate was open and he could smell autumn flowers.
3 Because he said the word correctly.
4 He died three months ago.
5 Because she looked like her mother.

Project work

1 Write about the life of women in England or your country at the time of the Brontës. Explain how things have changed.

2 Write a letter from Catherine to Heathcliff at the end of Chapter Five.

3 Imagine you are Cathy and you have married Linton. Write a diary about your time at Wuthering Heights.

4 Write Chapter Seven from *Wuthering Heights* as a play script.

An answer key for all questions and exercises can be found at **www.penguinreaders.co.uk**

Glossary

bare (adj.)
A *bare* room has nothing on the walls and nothing covering the floor.

beg (v.)
to ask someone to do something in a way that shows that you want it very much

betray (v.)
If you *betray* a person, you break a promise you made to them, or you tell other people about their secret.

bleed (v.)
If a part of your body *bleeds*, blood starts to come out of it.

blow (v.)
Wind *blows* when it moves strongly.

bruised (adj.)
If your skin is *bruised*, there are blue, yellow or brown marks on it (called *bruises*) because someone or something has hit it.

bury (v.)
to put a dead body under
the ground

cards (n.)
a game played with fifty-two
cards (= small pieces of strong
paper) with numbers and
pictures on them

carriage (n.)
A *carriage* has four wheels. People
sit in it, and a horse pulls it.

confused (adj.)
When you are *confused*, you
do not understand what
is happening.

cuckoo (n.)
a bird that puts its eggs in other
birds' *nests*. It makes a loud
call that sounds like its name.
In this story, Nelly thinks that
Heathcliff is like a *cuckoo*.

disturb (v.)
to wake someone who is sleeping

dresser (n.)
a tall piece of furniture for
keeping plates and cups

funeral (n.)
when people come together at a
church to *bury* a dead person

God (n.)
Many people believe that *God*
made this world and controls
everything that happens in it.

grave (n.)
the place in the ground where
a person is *buried*. Sometimes,
there is a large stone there with
the person's name on it.

grief (n.)
You feel *grief* when you are very
sad because someone has died.

groan (v.)
to make a long, low sound.
People *groan* when they are in
pain or when they have heard
some bad news.

growl (v.)
A dog *growls* when it makes a
long, low sound to show that it
does not want you to come
near it.

guest-house (n.)
a small hotel or someone's
home where you can pay
to stay the night

health (n.)
the way your body feels. If you
feel well, you are in good *health*.
If you feel ill, you are in
bad *health*.

heaven (n.)
Many people believe that, if you are a good person, you will go to *heaven* when you die.

housekeeper (n.)
a person who is paid to look after someone's home

jug (n.)
You put water, milk or wine in a *jug*. You use it to put a drink into a person's glass.

landlord (n.)
a person who owns a house where you live or stay. You pay the landlord, and then you can use the house or a room in the house.

lantern (n.)
a glass box with a light in it. You can carry a *lantern*. Then you can see while it is dark.

ledge (n.)
a long, narrow piece of wood along the wall below a window. You can put things on a *ledge*.

lonely (adj.)
You feel *lonely* when you are sad because you are alone or because you have no friends.

lost (adj.)
You are *lost* when you do not know where you are, and you cannot find the right path.

medicine (n.)
You take *medicine* to make you better when you are ill.

moody (adj.)
A *moody* person is often sad or angry.

moor (n.)
a large area of hills and grass. There are not many trees or houses on a *moor*.

nest (n.)
Birds live in a *nest*. They lay their eggs and look after their babies there.

part (v.)
to stop two people or things from being together

poor (adj.)
You say that someone is *poor* when you feel sad for them, for example, a *poor* child.

power (n.)
If you have *power*, you can tell people what to do, and they will do it.

revenge (n.)
You get *revenge* on someone when you do something to hurt them because they did something to hurt you.

rough (adj.)
not soft. People who work outside often have *rough* hands.

scratch (v.)
to make a thin mark with your fingernail (= one of the hard parts on the ends of your fingers)

servant (n.)
a person whose job is to cook and clean in someone's home

sir (n.)
a word that you use to talk to a man in a polite way

slim (adj.)
A *slim* person is thin in a healthy way.

soul (n.)
Many people believe that the *soul* is the part of a person that continues after they die.

spoiled (adj.)
A *spoiled* child always gets the things they want from their parents. They get angry when they do not get what they want.

tease (v.)
to make someone angry for fun

temper (n.)
Someone with a bad *temper* often gets very angry.

tenant (n.); **tenancy** (n.)
A *tenant* is a person who pays to live in someone's house. When you agree to pay to live in someone's house, this is a *tenancy*.

trick (v.)
If someone *tricks* you, they tell you something that is not true, and you believe them.

weak (adj.)
not strong

will (n.)
a document that gives information about who will get your money or things after you die

wine (n.)
a red or white drink made from grapes. People get drunk if they drink too much of it.

Yorkshire (pr. n.)
a place in the north of England. There are *moors* in some parts of *Yorkshire*.

Penguin Readers

Visit **www.penguinreaders.co.uk**
for FREE Penguin Readers resources
and digital and audio versions of this book.